NEW HAMPSHIRE

A Picture Book to Remember Her by

CRESCENT BOOKS
NEW YORK

CLB 1751
© 1987 Colour Library Books Ltd, Godalming, Surrey, England.
All rights reserved.
This 1991 edition published by Crescent Books,
distributed by Outlet Book Company, Inc, a Random House Company,
225 Park Avenue South, New York, New York 10003.
Printed in Hong Kong.
ISBN 0 517 62517 0
8 7 6 5 4 3 2

Though regarded by many as typically bucolic New England, New Hampshire has the fourth-largest proportion of factory workers in the country. It is also the fastest-growing state, except for Florida, east of the Mississippi River. Particularly in the south, it is a land of garish shopping malls, high technology industrial plants and condominium developments that are squeezing out some of its quaint New England-style towns.

It is conservative politically, with the result that it is, along with Alaska, unique among the 50 states in not having either a sales tax or an income tax. It is also in the bottom ten in spending for education, for prisons or for welfare.

The philosophy is that the towns, and not the state, and certainly not the Federal Government, should take care of such things. It has been a New Hampshire article of faith since Colonial times. At the beginning of the Revolutionary War, it found itself the only New England state still loyal to the Crown and the only one run directly from England. By the end of the War, when there was no more British authority in this part of North America, New Hampshire still hadn't organized its own government. In the confusion, the towns took over and became so powerful in state affairs that, when a legislature was formed, it was organized to include one member for each town regardless of its size. Today, they still operate that way in New Hampshire and it has the third-largest legislative body in the English speaking world. The other two are the United States Congress and the British House of Commons.

But if its government is peculiar compared to most other states, it was not for nothing that the poet Robert Frost once said "It is restful just to think about New Hampshire." It is a place of fast-moving rivers and deep forests, of majestic granite mountains and restful lakes surrounded by fragrant pines. It is the home state of Daniel Webster, one of the most respected United States Senators in the history of the country, ironically elected by the people of Massachusetts, his adopted state.

Many Americans get an intimate look at New Hampshire every four years when the race for the Presidency begins there in early March. Though the media swears it isn't all that important, that doesn't stop them from braving the cold to troop around the Granite State testing the icy waters to find out who's going to be eliminated from the race in the first Presidential Primary of the year. It all began with the first primaries established right before the First World War. New Hampshire set an early date to beat the spring thaw and its inevitable mud. Over the years, other states have changed their laws to make them first, but the New Hampshire Legislature is always ready to move the date back further if necessary. After all, it's a boost to the economy and outsiders do contribute mightily to the cost of running New Hampshire.

Facing page: Squam Lake, the second largest lake in New Hampshire.

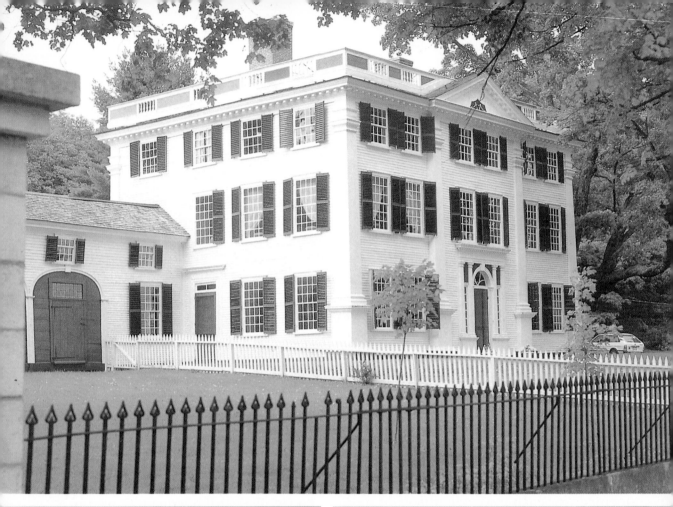

Left: the delicate, white-spired United Church of Christ in Keene, (above) spacious Manchester houses with wide balconies and (top) 19th-century Barrett House, a handsome Federal mansion in New Ipswich. Facing page: (top) sandy Hampton Beach, (center) a grand hotel near Hampton and (bottom) an inlet at Portsmouth.

New Hampshire's short stretch of coastline (these pages) is guarded by lighthouses and served by Portsmouth (above, left and overleaf), New Hampshire's only major seaport, set on the banks of the Piscataqua River.

Previous pages: (left top) Wentworth-Coolidge Mansion near Portsmouth, (left bottom) Prescott Park, (right center) a lobster hut on Sagamore Bridge and (remaining pictures) the restored Strawbery Banke settlement, Portsmouth. Left: Gilmanton, (top left) Rochester Jr. High School, (above) Old Colby Academy, New London, and (top) the Franklin Pierce Homestead, Hillsboro. Facing page: Shaker Village, Canterbury.

Previous pages: central Concord. Facing page: (top left) Sunapee harbor, (top right) Claremont, (center left and bottom left) Dartmouth College, near Hanover, (left) a mansion in Laconia and (remaining pictures) Wolfeboro.

17

The lakes region (these pages) of New Hampshire is made up of over a hundred lakes. It is a favorite spot with vacationers, who return there year after year to hunt the forests, fish the lakes and explore by boat the vast concentration of inland waterways. Squam Lake (previous pages and facing page top) still bears its Indian name and lies at the north end of Winnipesaukee Lake, surrounded by dense, green forest. Above and facing page bottom: Copps Pond, situated to the northwest of Mirror Lake (right).

Facing page: a pink and white house in the central White Mountains area. Above: a white clapboard house, (top) a farmhouse and (top left) a tree-lined road, near Sandwich. Left: fall colors at Whittier. Overleaf: (left) ski-runs at Waterville Valley ski resort, and (right) an aerial view of a covered bridge near Waterville Village. Following pages: the sun-dappled Swift River near Conway.

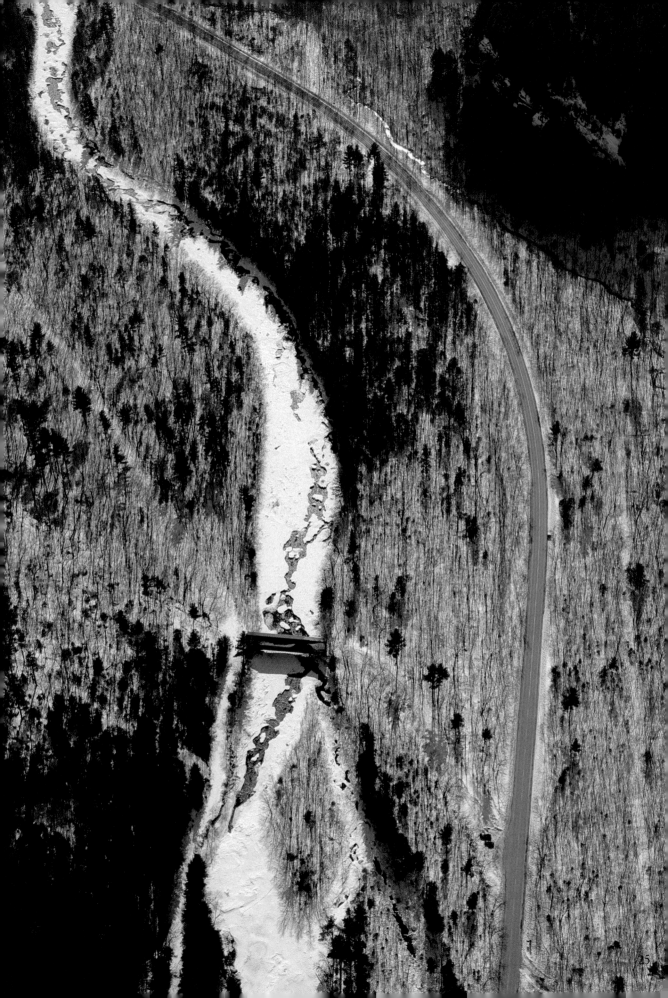

The aptly-named Swift River (overleaf right) flows through the Rocky Gorge Scenic Area (above and top) near Passaconaway, and (facing page bottom) beside the Kancamagus Highway, in White Mountain National Forest (right and overleaf left). Facing page top: Echo Lake near North Conway.

Built in 1874, the Russian-inspired railway station at North Conway (these pages) is now a museum and ticket office for the Conway Scenic Railroad.

These pages: two of the state's popular ski resorts. Above and top: Bretton Woods, which provides both Alpine and cross-country skiing, and (remaining pictures) Attitash, which, in addition to skiing, offers an Alpine slide and waterslides.

Top: the Saco River at Limington and (left) at Crawford Notch (previous pages). Above: a lakes-region heron and (facing page) Glen Ellis Falls. Overleaf: the Union Church and covered bridge at Stark.

Previous pages: (right) Whitneys Inn and (left top) a
forest home, Jackson, and (left bottom) the Ellis
River Valley. Top: Mt. Washington Hotel, in White
Mountain National Forest (remaining pictures).
Overleaf: (right bottom) a tarn on Mt. Washington,
which is climbed by the Cog Railway (remaining   45
pictures).

Previous pages: horses in the White Mountains (right), where the magnificent Mt. Washington Hotel (top and facing page bottom) stands at Bretton Woods. The Mt. Washington Cog Railway (above) and the Auto Road (facing page top) are easy ways of reaching the summit of Mt. Washington.

Previous pages: White Mountains scenery. Among the state's ski areas are Bretton Woods (below and right), Attitash (bottom right) and Wildcat Mountain (bottom and facing page). Overleaf: White Mountain National Forest seen from Sugar Hill Lookout.

Facing page: the white weatherboard Episcopal Church of St. Mathew at Sugar Hill. Left: fall colors at the vacation resort of Indian Head, and (above) the Sentinel Pine Covered Bridge at Franconia Notch, a deep valley some 6,500 acres in area set between the Franconia and Kinsman mountain ranges. Among the natural attractions of Franconia Notch are the Flume (overleaf left), a deep, narrow granite chasm, and Middle Kinsman Falls (overleaf right), fast-flowing over steep, 40-foot-high ledges on Cascade Brook.

Above: the Sentinel Pine Covered Bridge, overlooking a natural pool at Franconia Notch (top). Right and facing page: White Lake State Park.